Tips For The Sophisticated Marketer

How To Get A Big Payoff With A Small Internet Advertising Investment
2014 Version

DeAnna Troupe

Tips For The Sophisticated Marketer
DeAnna Troupe

Published by:
DeAnna Troupe

http://www.learnsmallbusiness.com

Table of Contents

Testimonials

It is all too easy for newcomers to online marketing to become scattered by attempting to be everywhere at once. Ms. Troupe brings focus to the reader by defining activities which can be done for little or no cost and the proposed benefits. Her tips are applicable to both entrepreneurs and writers as they attempt to build a platform and market their goods and services. Yes...you really can get there from here.--Jane C.

This book is meant for someone new to marketing. Someone who has just started a business either online or offline. However I found it a refreshing review and it reminded me of things I had forgotten over the years.

Ms. DeAnna Troupe offers tips for promoting your business both online and offline many for free and others for under $35. She first explains terminology that might be new to someone who has not been involved in marketing before. She then goes on in chapter after chapter giving suggestions for how to market your business giving concrete examples and how to go about placing ads locally and on the internet. She includes lists of addresses, name to search for, how to partner with other businesses, how to be creative in your marketing, she actually teaches you how to think outside of the box.

At the end of the book she includes links to her website and how to contact her if you have questions or are in need of assistance or unclear on anything in the book.

All in all I give this book 5 stars and would highly recommend her book to anyone starting a business who is overwhelmed with where to start in promoting their business or to anyone who needs a quick refresher after being out of the workforce for a while. --Tasha T.

Dedication

I want to thank my sweet, supportive husband for the love and support he gave me while I was working on this book.

I also want to thank all of the advertisers that contributed resources to this book. I couldn't have done it without them.

Bonus

As a thank you for purchasing this book, I have a bonus ecourse that I would LOVE for you to have. It's got even more information designed to help you promote your business with a small budget. This ecourse has 4 lessons with a wrap up email at the end of the 4 lessons. When you sign up for the ecourse, you will get a confirmation email. Be sure to confirm your email address. You may need to check your spam folder for it. The lessons will come from deanna@learnsmallbusiness.com so be sure to add that to your address book. To claim your bonus ecourse go to: http://www.learnsmallbusiness.com/bonus-ecourse-tfsm/ and fill out the form on this page. This page is password protected. The password is VIP2014 (all caps).

Disclaimer

The publisher and the author disclaim any
personal liability, loss, or
risk incurred as a result of the use of any
information or advice
contained herein, either directly or indirectly.
Furthermore, the publisher and author do not
guarantee that the
holder of this information will make profit from
the information
contained herein.
All mention of promises to make money, either
implied or not implied
is strictly based on the author's opinion of the
information contained
herein.
As with any business, it is up to the individual
owner of said business
to ensure the success of the business. You may
make more or less
than the program may or may not claim
herein.
It is strongly recommended that the purchaser
contact any and all
federal, state, and local agencies which may
regulate, tax, or
otherwise control the commencement of a
business such as the one
presented here.
The Publisher and Author do not intend to
render legal, accounting,

or other professional advice in the documents contained herein. Also please be advised that the Internet changes rapidly. Any information contained in this book is confirmed to be accurate as of the date is was published. Be sure to follow my blog at http://www.learnsmallbusiness.com for updates related to this book and affordable online advertising.

Introduction

The purpose of this book is to assist people with low budgets in their advertising efforts. This book is designed to teach people who are new to the Internet how to go about advertising their business with little money so some of these methods may seem kind of old to those of you who have been at this for a while.

I was getting annoyed with the high cost of advertising, so I decided to do some research to find out if there were places online that still had reasonably priced advertising. In my book reasonably priced is $35 USD or less. That is per ad, not per thousand. To my surprise I found several. The list of resources that you see here is not even close to an inclusive list.

I also decided to include a few articles related to on and offline advertising. If you would like to receive notices when this book is updated, be sure to visit my blog at http://www.learnsmallbusiness.com for updates.

Starting with the 2012 version, I have also added offline opportunities that cost $35 or less. The reason I did this is because you need to be anywhere your potential clients could be. Your website needs to be in magazines that your potential clients read. You need to be featured on radio shows your potential clients are listening to. So you'll find those opportunities here as well.

This book may contain affiliate links. I will get a commission if you purchase anything from these links.

How To Get Free Publicity For Your Business

Okay we're going to assume that you've already picked out what type of business you're going to run. I'm also going to assume that you already have a website up and running. The next thing that you need for your business is traffic. One way to get traffic to your website is through free publicity.

Would you like to expand the volume of your business? You can let thousands know about your service, your store, or your new product without spending a penny. Whether you want to make more sales or get an offer on television, you can broaden the scope of your clients by free publicity.

You don't have to climb a flagpole or hire a dancing bear to get attention.
In fact, with just a telephone, flyers, and some follow up letters, you can be making much more money than you are now.

What product or what business are you involved with that needs more customers? You might have a neighborhood store or you may have invented something that is difficult to market. Maybe you've launched a new web site.

How are you presently getting customers? Maybe you're advertising in trade journals, magazines, or newspapers. Perhaps you're doing banner swaps or participating in co-op programs with other ezine publishers.

Perhaps you're an author, trying to market his or her new book. Or maybe you're a young comic or an actor trying to establish his/her career.

Regardless of your business or enterprise, whether it is an online or an offline business, free publicity is available for you. Furthermore, you don't need any special training to do it. Take a look at the variety of options available to you.

What is Publicity?
Before we get into the different types of publicity out there, it would help if we knew what we were talking about. Publicity is making something known to the public, spreading information to the general, local, or national market. It is information with a news value used to attract popular opinion or support. Everybody uses publicity. Politicians, manufacturers, celebrities all use publicity to gain attention and further their causes. Publicity isn't limited to large organizations.

Small committees and enterprises use the local newspapers to publicize events and endeavors.

Publicity differs from advertising because it is free. Although some organizations trade tickets or services for mention in a particular publication, generally publicity is newsworthy information that a publication produces. Good publicity is one of the best ways of letting people know you have a worthwhile business.

Do your research. Before you begin a publicity campaign, you should know the answer to the following questions:

What is the product or service I am promoting?
What is the radius of the market (local, city, state, country, and world)?
What do the customers want?
Where do the customers go to buy my product?
Are my buyers mostly online or offline?

Where to publicize
Depending on your product or service, you have a full gamut of
possibilities for advertising without paying. Deciding on the type of media is as important as knowing about your product and your customers.

If you want to publicize directly to the general public national publications, metropolitan newspapers and Sunday supplements are one way to tap into the market.

For a local enterprise, a profitable business, a charity, or community service- the local paper is the best source of free advertising. Don't go for the big fish first. Start with the local press and then work your way up.

Make it newsworthy
In order to qualify for publication, your story must be newsworthy.

Anything published in the newspapers, magazines, and trade journals must be of importance to its readers.

You may have a new product or product line that can be featured in the magazines.

If not, you need to come up with a unique angle. For example, you may have to come up with fresh ideas for your service.

Or maybe an unusual piece of information in the inventor or business owner's biography might make an interesting twist. One of the tools you will be using to get this publicity is the press release.

Formatting tips
Keep the press release to one page. It should be brief and informative.

Write the words For Release in full capital letters at the right. Make sure you include your daytime phone number, address, email address, and website address if you have one.

Write a personal letter to the editor.

Be cordial, but keep it short. If you have a product that you can mail, send the editor a sample if he or she agrees to that. Watch the publication and clip the press release when it is published.

Some other options include signature files, joint ventures, free for
all links, informational articles, webrings, and giveaways.
Signature files are great ways to get free publicity for your business. It's
just a short blurb at the end of your email. It's not considered spam. Of
course, you shouldn't just send blank emails to people, just so they'll see your signature file. That might be considered spam to some people.

Joint ventures are also great ways to get free publicity for your business.
Joint ventures are fairly easy to set up. Just find someone who is not in direct competition with you that may benefit from your book, product or service. Ask them if they will promote your product to their list in exchange for a link on your website or an announcement to your list.
Most business owners will agree to such an arrangement as this is a win-win for everyone.

Also, you can gain free publicity by writing informational articles. My suggestion is that you post these for free and include a resource box at the end of your article with your contact information and a short blurb about the product or service you are trying to promote.

You can also get free publicity for your business by appearing on Internet radio shows. People that host Internet radio shows are always looking for interesting guests to interview on their show. I host an Internet radio show myself and I can tell you from experience that it's a lot easier to do a radio talk show when you have a guest to interview than when you don't. Those days that I don't have a guest make me feel like I'm talking to myself.

One place to find Internet radio shows is BlogTalkRadio. There are numerous radio shows on various topics on BlogTalkRadio. All you have to do is sign up for a free membership by going to http://www.blogtalkradio.com and listening to archives of shows related to your topic. When you find shows you like, contact the host and tell them you like their show. Offer to be a guest on their show if they ever need one. Be sure to keep in touch with the host because sometimes we get busy and forget about people that we want to have on our show.
If you'd like to be on my show, you can go to http://www.blogtalkradio.com/deannatroupe.

You can also get free publicity for your product or services by using social media. The best way to use social media is to get to know people that are in your target market. Think of social media as one to one not one to many. Pick one or two people each day to hold an individual conversation with. Pretty soon you'll have a large number of people following you, interested in purchasing what you are selling.

Giveaways are an excellent way to get free publicity for your business.
You could give away a report, an e-book, or even a coupon for discounted
services. I will discuss each of these methods in more detail.

Using Social Media to Get Free Advertising For Your Business

Now I couldn't write a book about advertising online without mentioning social networking. Social networking is just like networking in person except you use a computer to meet new people. Social networking is something you've got to be doing or you'll miss out on lots of new potential clients.

There are literally thousands of social networking sites with more popping up everyday. I think you should only focus on a few to get started so you won't get overwhelmed. The sites you definitely should spend some time on are Twitter, LinkedIn, and Facebook.

Twitter is a microblogging site where you answer the question: "What are you doing?" several times a day in 140 characters or less. I know this seems like a waste of time, but it's a very powerful tool because you get a real time glimpse into the lives of your potential clients. The best way to find these clients is to go to http://search.twitter.com and type in a subject. You'll get so see who is talking about what you're interested in right at this moment. Twitter is also powerful because it allows you to let people see what makes you tick and show off your expertise. Just like with forums post useful links and answer people's questions. I've written a complete book with tips to help you master Twitter. It's called Tips About Twitter For The Sophisticated Marketer and it is available on Amazon's Kindle here: http://www.amazon.com/About-Twitter-Sophisticated-ebook/B007OKBVUW/. You can always get more information about twitter by following me at http://www.twitter.com/deannatroupe.

Another good social networking site to join is Facebook. You join Facebook by going to http://www.facebook.com. Once you join Facebook you should start searching for people you may have gone to school with or met at a face to face networking event. Facebook is kind of confusing at first. The best way to learn Facebook is just to jump in and play around with the tools. Upload your pictures and videos to your profile to share with your friends. One thing to know about Facebook is that they change the interface quite often at Facebook. Don't get too comfortable with one setup. As soon as you do, look for them to change it up. You have to be flexible when dealing with Facebook. You must be prepared to go with the flow as they say. Another top social media site is LinkedIn. LinkedIn is different from Facebook and Twitter in that it is more geared towards business than Twitter and Facebook. LinkedIn started off as a way for recruiters and job hunters to connect. It operates based on people inviting people in their real life network to join LinkedIn. The idea is that people will be able to recommend people they know for job openings and as service professionals. You can also set up a company profile and have people recommend you to be in the service directory. LinkedIn is similar to Facebook and Twitter in that you have to interact with people in order for it to work. You can't just go around adding contacts and never email that person. Don't just send the default LinkedIn invitation, either. That makes you appear lazy. Most people will decline such an invite. Instead of a canned invitation, mention something in that person's profile that interested you. Mention why you want to connect with that person. Tell them what you have to offer them. This type of invitation will get accepted quicker than one that is a default invitation.

Using Video To Get Free Advertising For Your Business

Another excellent way to get free advertising for your business is to use videos. Now I know what you're thinking, "I don't have a fancy video camera." So what? You don't need a fancy high tech video camera to make a video. Most digital cameras also record video. You can also create PowerPoint presentations and do screenshots. I recommend http://www.screencast-o-matic.com for this because it is free and you can use it online. You can record a demonstration of you using a software program that is critical to your field. You can record a motivational speech to show your clients. The possibilities are endless.

Once you record this video be sure to upload it to a video sharing site such as http://www.youtube.com because YouTube already has the traffic you're looking for. You just have to make your video a compelling one. Be sure to put your website url in your YouTube profile so people can find your website.

Be sure to tell your network about your video. This is especially important if there are a lot of bloggers in your network. If your video is about something they blog about, they may repost your video in their blog, thereby exposing you and your business to a whole different audience. Once again this costs you nothing as you have already made the video. You can also get free advertising for your business by using forums.

Using Forums To Get Free Advertising For Your Business

An excellent way to get free targeted advertising to your business is to actively participate in a forum related to your business. The reason forums are so effective is because the people that frequent the forums are already discussing the very thing that you're trying to solve with your business.

The best way to start using this method is to join a few forums related to your niche and start reading the discussions. You'll find people asking questions related to what it is you do. Don't just jump in and answer by posting a link to your website without giving the answer. This is considered spamming and you don't want to get accused of being a spammer. That is the quickest way to ruin your online reputation that you're working so hard to build up.
Be sure to read the rules of the forum before you post. Once you've become familiar with the rules, start answering questions that the members have. Also post questions that you may have. Be sure to visit the forums you choose at least once a day so people don't forget who you are.

Forums can be a great way to drive traffic to your website, just don't overdo it. It's really easy to get lost in a forum and just spend all your time posting and not getting anything else done. Don't fall into this trap. Allocate yourself a certain amount of time per day for forum marketing. Keep track of the time you spend on forum marketing. You don't want to spend all of your time on one method and overlook other methods that can generate traffic to your website.

Using Ezines, Reprint Articles, and Newsgroups To Generate Traffic To Your Website

Do you want to reach millions of potential customers for FREE? Well you can if you know how. The Internet, that massive network of thousands of computers around the world, also known as the "Information Super Highway," is your ticket to generating free leads and sales. You just have to make sure that you know who you want to advertise to and be where they hang out.

As with any other medium, there is a correct way and an incorrect way to advertise online. One correct way is to post your message to various newsgroups that welcome advertising. If you dig around, I'm sure you'll find a couple of newsgroups that fit this description. Posting your ad to these newsgroups is a good way to start your advertising campaign because they are seen by millions and it didn't cost you a dime. Your ad will last for about two weeks and then you will need to repost your ad. Keep track of your ad response and focus your efforts on the ads that bring you the best results.

27

Another source of free advertising is publishing articles that others can reprint freely. People such as webmasters and e-zine publishers are always in need of fresh content. Write about something you are interested in. If you have a certain area of expertise, write an article about that. Place a resource box at the end of your article with all of your pertinent contact information. Don't attempt to sell your product here. Do that when you get contacted for more information.

One more source of free advertising is ezines. Some ezines allow their subscribers to advertise for free. Different ezines have different rules regarding their advertising. There are a lot of directories online that list ezines that offer free advertising. Just go to any search engine and type in ezines and you should find a considerable amount of ezines listed.

You can also create what is known as a signature file. A signature file is a footer that goes at the bottom of any email that you send out. Your signature file contains information such as your company name, email address, and website. You should also include a short sales message in your signature file.

Now that you know the correct ways to advertise for free online, here are a few incorrect things to do when advertising online. Don't be tempted to post ads in any newsgroup that you see. Follow their posting rules to the letter. If they say NO ADVERTISING, don't advertise. This is a good way for you to get thrown out of the group. Additionally, don't write articles that serve as sales letters. Editors will spot this rather quickly and they will not publish your article. There are many places to advertise for free online. If you utilize them, you will be well on your way to building your business online.

Free Places to Submit Your Ezine Articles

Here are some sites that accept articles.

http://thephantomwriters.com
http://www.authorconnection.com/
http://www.ezinearticles.com
http://www.isnare.com
http://www.articlesbase.com/
http://www.hubpages.com
http://www.articlesbin.com/
http://www.ideamarketers.com
http://www.goarticles.com

Websites With Affordable or Free Advertising

Mom Pack

http://www.MomPack.com

Moms Promoting Moms For Free

The Mom Pack Mission ... to support our mutual goals of success through an innovative, free advertising partnership.

Home Biz Moms

http://www.home-biz-moms.com

This site is geared towards work at home moms. It is chock full of resources aimed at helping moms that want to work from home. If your product is something that will appeal to this crowd, then you might want to check this site out.

Christian Mommies

http://www.christian-mommies.com/

This site is aimed at moms that are Christian. Be careful about what you promote on this site. You wouldn't want to promote anything questionable to this group.

Gone Clicking

http://www.goneclicking.com

This is a site where you get credits for surfing other people's websites. These credits allow you to display your site to other people. This is another place for a squeeze page because the people looking at your site are not going to stay on your site very long because they want to get to the next site.

Two Bucks An Ad
(Affiliate Link)

http://www.learnsmallbusiness.com/suggests/2bucksanad/

This is a good place to buy affordable ezine advertising.

My Wizard Ads

http://www.learnsmallbusiness.com/suggests/mwa

This is an affiliate link (not an Amazon Affiliate link).
This is a great place to find affordable ezine advertising.

IM Hot Spot http://www.imhotspot.com
This is good if your product or service is something that would be of interest to Internet Marketers. There is a section for you to post your offer for free. You can also share your free special offers here.

Five And Ten Marketing With Dryer Buzz
http://www.dryerbuzz.com/promo/five-and-ten-marketing-with-dryerbuzz/

Web Classifieds

http://www.webclassifieds.us

This is a free classifieds site. You can post your ad here for free. There are also other options available if you want to pay for them.

Radio Station With Affordable Advertising

PharohShus, LLC
For PR/sponsorship opportunities contact
Jennifer Robinsion
email: booking@pharohshus.com
Phone: 678-596-2785
Website: http://www.pharoahshus.com
This is for an actual radio station in Metro
Atlanta. Contact the person listed in this book
and ask what the current rates are.

Other Books By DeAnna Troupe

Tips About Twitter For The Sophisticated Marketer

7 Tips For The Sophisticated Freelancer

These books are both available on Amazon or by contacting me.

About The Author

DeAnna Troupe is a native of Atlanta, Georgia, and a serial entrepreneur that has always loved helping others. Her very first job was as an algebra tutor at the tender age of 14. Since then she has amassed over 10 years of experience at all levels of business including running her own freelance secretarial business for 5 years. She has been on the social media scene since before we even knew that's what we were doing. She has a knack for coming up with creative ways to solve tough problems. She is an effective teacher that enjoys seeing her clients get to the next level with their business. When she's not coaching clients on integrating video in their social media strategy, she enjoys spending time with her husband

and kids. She also enjoys reading, writing, crocheting, singing, playing cards, and playing board games.

Ways To Contact The Author

Blog: http://www.learnsmallbusiness.com
Facebook:
http://www.facebook.com/deannatroupecoach
Twitter: http://www.twitter.com/deannatroupe
Email: deanna@learnsmallbusiness.com

Be sure to leave a review on Amazon if you enjoyed this book. Also if you write about this in your blog, please send me a link. Here is where you go to leave your review:
http://www.amazon.com/Sophisticated-Marketer-Advertising-Investment-ebook/dp/B007G480J6/

www.ingramcontent.com/pod-product-compliance
Lightning Source LLC
Chambersburg PA
CBHW041151180526
45159CB00002BB/776